Living Green

BILLINGS COUNTY PUBLIC SCHOOL
Box 307
Medora, North Dakota 58645

by Helen Orme

Consultant: Terry Jennings, Ph.D.
Educational Consultant

BEARPORT
PUBLISHING

New York, New York

Credits

Cover and Title Page, © Dietrich Rose/zefa/Corbis; Credit Page, © Markus Gann/Shutterstock; 4–5, © Goodman Photography/Shutterstock; 6, © iofoto/Shutterstock; 6–7, © J Marshall/Tribaleye Images/Alamy; 8–9, © John Terence Turner/Alamy; 9, © Joy Brown/Shutterstock; 10, © floydian/Shutterstock; 10–11, © Paul Cooper/Rex Features; 12–13, © Paul Paladin/Shutterstock; 13, © Carrie Bottomley/iStockphoto; 14, © Péter Gudella/Shutterstock; 14–15, © Shi Yali/Shutterstock; 16, © Sally Scott/Shutterstock; 16–17, © spe/Shutterstock; 18, © Thinkstock Images/Jupiterimages; 18–19, © Michael Piazza/Jupiterimages; 20, © Terrance Emerson/Shutterstock; 20–21, © Joe Sohm/Digital Vision/Photolibrary Group; 22–23, © Otmar Smit/Shutterstock; 24T, © Mandy Godbehear/Shutterstock; 24B, © Deniz/Shutterstock; 25, © Alexander Studentschnig/Shutterstock; 27, © Janine Wiedel Photolibrary/Alamy; 28T, © Roger Whiteway/iStockphoto; 28B, © Raffi Alexander/iStockphoto; 29T, © Brand X Pictures/Jupiterimages; 29B, © Meggj/Shutterstock; 30, © Kenneth V. Pilon/Shutterstock.

Every effort has been made to trace the copyright holders, and we apologize in advance for any unintentional omissions. We would be pleased to insert the appropriate acknowledgments in any subsequent edition of this publication.

The Earth in Danger series is printed on recycled paper.

Library of Congress Cataloging-in-Publication Data

Orme, Helen.
    Living green / by Helen Orme.
        p. cm. — (Earth in danger)
    Includes bibliographical references and index.
    ISBN-13: 978-1-59716-728-4 (library binding)
    ISBN-10: 1-59716-728-2 (library binding)
    1. Environmental protection—Citizen participation—Juvenile literature. 2. Sustainable living—Juvenile literature. I. Title.

    TD171.7.O76 2009
    640—dc22
                                2008022250

Contents

Living Green

Each year, farmers plant seeds that grow into fruits, vegetables, and other crops. These seeds and the plants they grow into are **renewable resources**—we won't run out of them because there is a new crop every year. Many other natural resources, such as water, wind, and sunlight, are also renewable.

Some resources, however, will eventually run out. These nonrenewable resources include oil and metals **mined** from the ground. Living in a way that uses as few nonrenewable resources as possible is called **sustainable living**—or living green.

Today, about 91 percent of the power used in the United States comes from nonrenewable resources—oil, coal, gas, and nuclear. Less than 9 percent comes from renewable energy sources, such as sunlight, water, and wind.

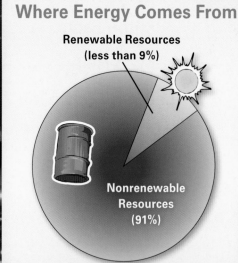

Where Energy Comes From

Renewable Resources
(less than 9%)

Nonrenewable
Resources
(91%)

To live in a sustainable way, people must use fewer nonrenewable resources to power their homes, offices, cars, and appliances.

More People, More Things!

Today's incredible **technology** produces many goods, such as cell phones, electronic games, and flat-screen TVs, that could barely have been imagined in the past. As technology advances and the world's population increases, demand for these goods will also increase.

It takes many natural resources, mostly nonrenewable ones, to make these things. The challenge now is to figure out how to cut back on using nonrenewable resources by finding more sustainable ways of producing goods, food, fuel, and shelter.

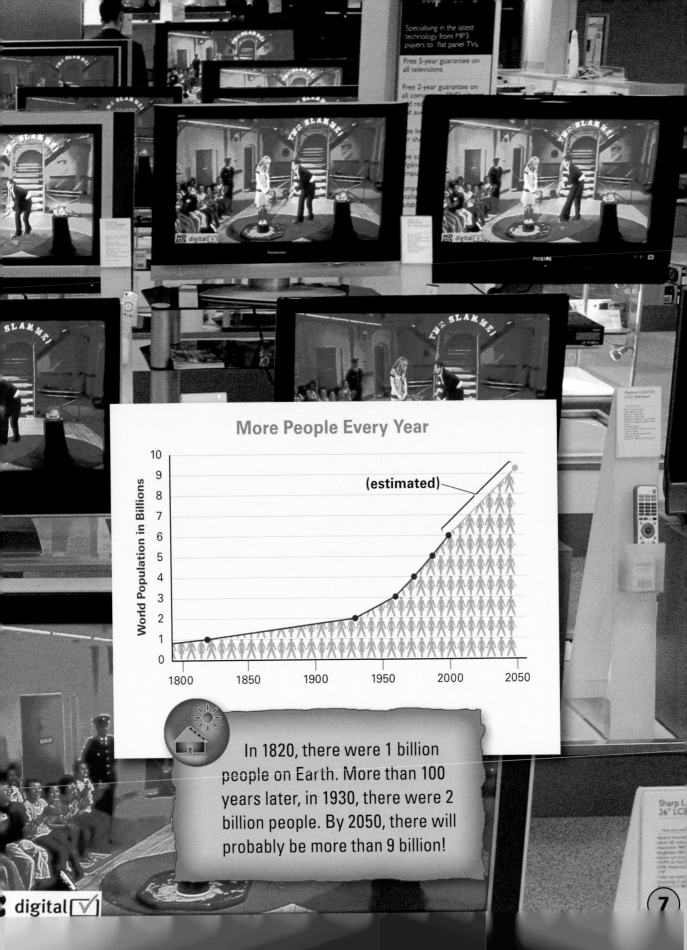

More People Every Year

World Population in Billions

(estimated)

1800 1850 1900 1950 2000 2050

In 1820, there were 1 billion people on Earth. More than 100 years later, in 1930, there were 2 billion people. By 2050, there will probably be more than 9 billion!

digital ☑

The Problems with Fossil Fuels

Much of the energy used to produce the goods people use every day comes from burning oil, coal, and gas. These nonrenewable resources are called **fossil fuels**. They formed from the remains of plants and animals that died up to 300 million years ago. Unfortunately, the process that creates these fuels takes so long that once the present supplies are gone, there will be no way to get more.

Yet people keep burning oil, coal, and gas for most of their energy. In fact, 85 percent of the power people use comes from fossil fuels. As these fuels are burned, air **pollution** gets worse and the gases that trap heat in Earth's **atmosphere** build up.

Greenhouse gases, such as **carbon dioxide**, are in the smoke that results from burning fossil fuels. The gases work like the glass in a greenhouse—they let in warmth from the sun, but they trap a lot of the heat inside our atmosphere. Many scientists think these gases are causing our **climate** to change and become warmer. This heating up of air and water temperatures is called **global warming**.

A greenhouse

As Earth's climate gets warmer, glaciers around the world, such as this one in Alaska, are melting.

Low-Energy Buildings

Most buildings use a lot of energy to heat and cool air. Unfortunately, some of the air escapes through walls and windows, wasting the power used to treat it. Low-energy buildings, however, are different. They are **insulated** to make sure that most of the treated air stays inside the buildings.

Low-energy buildings often take advantage of the sun to provide heat. Some structures use solar panels to heat water and air. Other buildings simply have large windows to let in sunlight for both light and heat.

Buildings use 40 percent of all the energy produced in the United States.

The solar panels on this home use energy from the sun to heat air and water.

What's in the Trash?

More than 60 percent of the things people throw away can be **recycled**. Newspapers, for example, can be used to make "new" paper.

Recycling cuts down on wastes that often pollute the environment. For example, bringing aluminum cans to a recycling center keeps the cans out of a **landfill**. It also cuts down on energy use and pollution. How? Manufacturing new cans from old ones uses 95 percent less energy and causes 95 percent less pollution than making new cans from other raw materials.

One of the best ways to save resources is to simply reuse items. For example, a plastic bag from the grocery store can be used over and over. Then, when it tears, it can go to the recycling plant.

Recycling containers for glass, paper, and plastic

Recycling two glass bottles saves enough energy to make five cups of tea or coffee!

Travel Smart

Just as reusing items **conserves** materials, saves energy, and cuts down on air pollution, making travel plans carefully does the same thing. Every year, many people go on vacations far from their homes. Often they travel in airplanes. Unfortunately, an airplane produces more greenhouse gases than a car, bus, or train.

Living green means choosing ways to travel that use the least power and cause the least pollution. Planning vacations close to home, driving more energy-efficient small cars, and using air travel only when necessary reduces pollution and energy use.

One round-trip flight of 1,600 miles (2,575 km) puts 720 pounds (327 kg) of carbon dioxide into the atmosphere—that's about the same weight as four adults.

Traveling in a train is much better for the environment than flying in a plane or driving in a car because a train produces much less carbon dioxide.

Water, Our Most Precious Resource

Freshwater is used for drinking, washing, cooking, growing food, and getting rid of waste. It is essential for all life. Luckily, water is a renewable resource. In many places, however, freshwater is being used faster than it can be replaced by rainfall. To make sure this resource is always available, people must do everything possible to avoid wasting it.

Communities are finding many ways to cut back on water use. For example, they are asking homeowners to install low-flow showerheads and low-flush toilets. Both of these devices reduce water use. Some companies are also recycling wastewater by purifying it. This water is then used for crops.

Crop irrigation accounts for 70 percent of the world's freshwater use.

Thinking Locally

Until the twentieth century, people got most food and other goods from their communities. If they needed potatoes or grain, for example, they grew it themselves or bought it from **local** farmers.

Today, the food and other goods in our homes come from all over the world. Shipping and packaging these items uses lots of energy. Food also has to be preserved—often with refrigeration—as it moves from farms to places around the world, which uses even more energy.

When people buy items produced locally, they are really saving precious resources. Less transportation energy is needed to bring the items to market. Also, simpler packaging is required as the goods are being moved over short distances.

Some adults drive many miles to get to work. Phones, computers, and other machines, however, make it possible for people to work from home, reducing the amount of fuel they use for transportation.

Food for Thought

What people choose to eat also affects nonrenewable resources. For example, a lot of energy is needed to raise food for farm animals. Growing the grain—mostly corn—that cows, pigs, chickens, and other animals eat takes fuel to run machines that plant, **harvest**, and water the grain. Then more fuel is used to transport it to market. Is this a good use of resources that are in limited supply?

If people ate less meat, the grain used to raise animals could be used for people. Some scientists estimate that the grain used to feed animals in the United States each year, for example, could feed 800 million people!

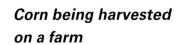

Corn being harvested on a farm

Farm animals eat 70 percent of the grain grown in the United States.

The Future

Nonrenewable resources, such as oil and gas, are in limited supply. So they must be used wisely. Once the resources are gone, it will be impossible for people to sustain the way they live now—using fossil fuels to power cars, airplanes, power plants, and so on.

Fortunately, scientists are always finding new ways to provide power for people. Today, more and more power is being made with sustainable sources of energy such as sunlight and wind. Eventually, these new ways will greatly reduce the use of fossil fuels.

In the meantime, it's important to remember that cutting back on the energy used now means that resources will last longer. It also means that people in the future will also have some of these precious resources to use themselves.

The cells on this house's roof turn the sun's energy into electricity without making air pollution.

In 1955, the world used about 850 million tons (771 million metric tons) of oil every year. Today, it uses almost 4 billion tons (3.6 billion metric tons) of oil per year. That means the world today is using almost five times more oil each year than it did just a little more than half a century ago.

Oil Use over the Years

1955   2008

 = 100 million tons
(90.7 million metric tons)

Saving Water

Follow these tips to save water at home:

- Do not use a hose when washing the car or watering the garden. Use a bucket of water or a watering can instead. This will make it easier to control exactly how much water is used.

- Save the water used to wash vegetables for watering plants.

- Take showers instead of baths. They use less water.

- Wash dishes by hand. Dishwashers use lots of water and power!

- Fix leaky taps.

- Fill a plastic bottle with water and put it in the toilet tank. The bottle will take up space so less water is needed to fill the tank.

Saving Energy

Follow these tips to save energy at home:

- When not using computers or TVs, turn them off.
- Never waste hot water by letting the tap run.
- When the weather is cool, turn the indoor heat down and wear more clothes inside.
- When the weather is warm, turn off the air conditioner; dress in cool, loose-fitting clothes; and open up some windows. Using fresh air for cooling saves energy.
- When adults are buying new equipment, such as washing machines and vacuum cleaners, ask them to check product labels to see how energy-efficient the machines are.

Dry clothes on a clothesline or on an indoor clothes rack. Tumble dryers use lots of energy.

BILLINGS COUNTY PUBLIC SCHOOL
Box 307
Medora, North Dakota 58645

Zero-Carbon House

When fossil fuels such as oil, natural gas, and coal are burned, they give off a gas called carbon dioxide. This greenhouse gas stops heat from escaping into space, which many scientists believe is causing global warming.

A zero-carbon building is constructed to use little energy and produce no greenhouse gases. It is highly energy-efficient and will not contribute to global warming. How does it do this? A zero-carbon house uses no fossil fuels, so it does not produce carbon dioxide. It also does not use electricity from power stations. Instead, it uses renewable resources like wind, water, and sunlight to produce electricity.

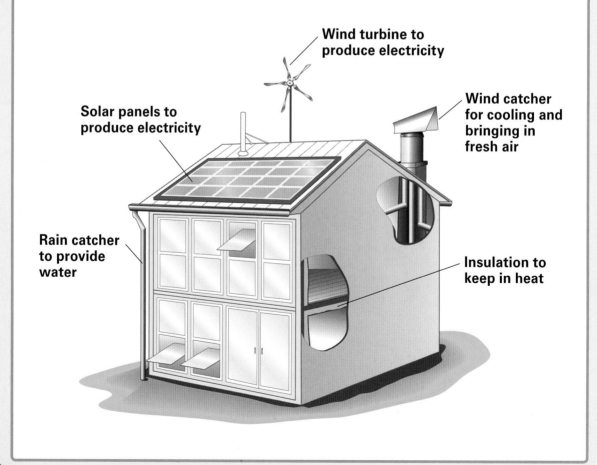

Wind turbine to produce electricity

Wind catcher for cooling and bringing in fresh air

Solar panels to produce electricity

Rain catcher to provide water

Insulation to keep in heat

Eating Green

To eat in a more sustainable way, try some of these ideas for healthier dining:

- Buy **organic foods** at least some of the time. These foods have been produced in a sustainable way, without the use of **pesticides** and **chemical fertilizers**. Some people believe organic food tastes better than food grown in other ways.

- Buy food that is grown nearby. A trip to a vegetable stand or farmers market—which sells locally-grown fruits and vegetables—is the best way to get the freshest food. It also reduces the demand for items produced in a nonsustainable way.

- Eat less meat and more fresh fruit and vegetables. If people make this switch, there will be less demand for meat—so less grain will be used for animal feed.

- Plant a small garden or window box. Herbs, lettuce, radishes, and baby carrots can be grown in small spaces.

The Plastic Bag—A Case Study

Using plastic bags is not a sustainable way to carry items because the bags are made from oil, a fossil fuel. Making these bags not only uses up nonrenewable resources, it also adds more carbon dioxide to Earth's atmosphere.

The plastic bags themselves cause serious pollution problems on land and in water. More than 500 billion plastic bags are made each year, and many of them end up as litter. Here are some ways to reduce the use of these bags:

- Write to your representatives in Congress. Tell them that if the government passes laws requiring stores to charge money for plastic bags, people will use fewer of them.

- Always take a shopping bag to the store and reuse it as many times as possible.

- Don't buy shopping bags made from plastic. Buy bags made from paper, cotton, and other sustainable materials.

- Place used plastic bags in trash cans for recyclable plastics or return them to the store.

Reusing

One of the most important ways to save resources is to reuse old things. Here are some tips:

- Donate old clothes to charities. They can be used by someone who needs them.

- Cut up worn-out clothes and use them for dusting or cleaning cars.

- Make things out of used plastic tubs—the kind that cottage cheese, margarine, and other foods come in. Decorate them and fill them full of presents at birthdays and holidays; use them to store small items; store leftovers in them; and so on.

- Make greeting cards with pictures cut out from old magazines or used birthday and holiday cards.

- Make new meals from leftovers—never throw food away unless it's spoiled.

How to Help

Everyone needs to get involved in living green. Here are some things to do:

- Copy the tips on saving energy from page 25 and post them in the kitchen. See how good each family member is at following the tips.

- Don't buy water in plastic bottles. Use tap water. Producing, bottling, and transporting water bottles releases 600 times more greenhouse gases into the atmosphere than getting water from the tap.

- Do a school energy check. First make a checklist of ways to save energy. Then see how good students and teachers are at saving power. For example: Are lights turned off in rooms that aren't being used? Are computers left on sleep mode or turned off when not in use? Are rooms too warm in the winter? Are there water leaks anywhere in or around the school building?

- Become plugged into the clean-water network! Support the work of water charities around the world. Visit **www.wateraid.org** to find out what an international water charity does to bring safe, clean water to people all over the world. Find out how to become better informed about fighting illness and poverty through clean-water organizations worldwide.

Learn More Online

To learn more about living green, visit
www.bearportpublishing.com/EarthinDanger

Glossary

atmosphere (AT-muhss-fihr) the air and gases that surround Earth

carbon dioxide (KAR-buhn dye-OK-side) a greenhouse gas given off when fossil fuels are burned

chemical fertilizers (KEM-uh-kuhl FUR-tuh-*lize*-urz) plant food that is made from chemicals

climate (KLYE-mit) patterns of weather over a long period of time

conserves (kuhn-SURVS) keeps in a safe condition; doesn't waste

fossil fuels (FOSS-uhl FYOO-uhlz) fuels such as coal, oil, and gas made from the remains of plants and animals that died millions of years ago

freshwater (FRESH-*wa*-tur) water that does not contain salt

global warming (GLOHB-uhl WORM-ing) the warming of Earth's air and oceans as a result of a buildup of greenhouse gases in the atmosphere

greenhouse gases (GREEN-*houss* GAS-iz) carbon dioxide, methane, and other gases that trap warm air in the atmosphere so it cannot escape into space; the gases responsible for global warming

harvest (HAR-vist) to collect or gather crops

insulated (IN-suh-*layt*-id) protected from losing heat, usually by some kind of barrier or wall

landfill (LAND-fill) a large hole in the ground that serves as a dumping ground for garbage

local (LOH-kuhl) having to do with the immediate area where one lives; a local business is one that would be near one's home

mined (MINDE) removed from inside Earth

organic foods (or-GAN-ik FOODZ) food grown without using chemical fertilizers or pesticides

pesticides (PESS-tuh-sidez) chemicals that kill insects and other pests that damage crops

pollution (puh-LOO-shuhn) harmful substances that are released into the environment (air, water, and soil)

recycled (ree-SYE-kuhld) when unwanted materials are turned into something useful

renewable resources (re-NOO-uh-buhl REE-sorss-iz) resources such as water, wind, and sunlight that are continuously renewed or replaced by natural processes

sustainable living (suh-STAYN-uh-buhl LIV-ing) a way of living that does not use up nonrenewable resources; living in a way that can be continued forever

technology (tek-NOL-uh-jee) the science of making useful things

Index

Read More

Amsel, Sheri. *The Everything Kids' Environment Book: Learn How You Can Help the Environment—By Getting Involved at School, at Home, or at Play.* Avon, MA: Adams Media (2007).

Roca, Núria. *The Three R's: Reuse, Reduce, Recycle.* Hauppauge, NY: Barron's Educational Series (2007).

Thornhill, Jan. *This Is My Planet: The Kids' Guide to Global Warming.* Toronto, Canada: Maple Tree Press (2007).